The Defense
of the
Mieza HChip

IP Strategy for Tech professionals

I0005634

Robert Cantrell

&

Duncan Bucknell

Think IP Strategy

www.thinkipstrategy.com

ISBN - 978-1-4478-9164-2

Contents

How to get more from this book

We've found that the most useful books in our professional lives are the ones that are well-thumbed, full of notes and always close to hand. We want you to get as much as possible out of this book and so we have left plenty of room for you to add your own notes on the pages. We have also provided notes sections at the end of each chapter and a summary notes section at the start of the book for you to collect your ideas so that you have a quick, personalized guide immediately to hand.

Please do share your thoughts and insights with us so that we can make the next edition even better.

Preface

In 1986, the Army introduced me to a short text written in 1903 that served as a primer for understanding strategy and tactics. This book, written by Major General Sir Ernest Swinton, carried with it the somewhat unusual title, *The Defence of Duffer's Drift*. The power of Sir Swinton's approach to teaching all the nuances of winning a small unit military action, however, has carried it through over a century of military education to this point.

Just as the main character in Sir Swinton's book faces many more ways to fail than to succeed, IP strategists also face an environment where plans can easily go awry. Much of this stems from the failure to appreciate the entirety of a competitive situation whereby even operating in accord with understood best IP practices, for example securing good patents, is not enough to win.

In this IP-based adaptation of *The Defence of Duffer's Drift*, here titled *The Defense of the Mieza HChip: IP Strategy for Tech Professionals*, a new Head of Intellectual Property for a small technology company has five dreams of discovery where his IP strategies fall short in the face of more astute competition until the sixth dream where he finally gets it right. The reasons for his failure rest both inside and outside the traditional responsibilities of the IP professional, but never beyond his potential sphere of influence.

Mieza, the name used in the title of this adaptation, was a village in Ancient Macedon where Aristotle educated Alexander the Great when he was a boy. Aristotle had a well-rounded background in literature, math, and science, the knowledge of which an intelligent strategist, like Alexander the Great, could make full use. In this story we incorporate central tenets of many professions that an IP strategist can draw upon to succeed.

Our hope is that this book, as an adaptation of Sir Swinton's primer, will allow IP strategists to discover opportunities and vulnerabilities of their own positions before the market puts them to test and while they can still do something positive about them. Here is a holistic insight into what it truly means to be strategic with IP.

Acknowledgements

We first acknowledge Major General Sir Ernest Swinton for his creative approach in 1903 to teaching nuances of strategy that are difficult to appreciate without reference to real causes and effects. He took to heart in his writing that people tend to learn faster how to succeed when they experience and survive the travails of failure. His approach in his book, *The Defence of Duffer's Drift*, from which this book is an adaptation, challenges the conventional notion of the singular case study review in strategy. He shows the depth of exploration often needed to assure that all the other things that can go wrong when executing a plan do not hide behind that which went wrong first.

We also thank our clients who have imparted to us ideas and the opportunities to address real time challenges including those represented in this book. We hope that by challenging their assumptions, we have made unnecessary many lessons that might otherwise have been learned the hard way. No amount of study can beat first-hand experiences to understand the subtlety behind strategic advantage in IP and to recognize the pitfalls that may only appear obvious in hindsight.

Summary notes

Prologue

As evening fell after a long and tiring day, I, arrived at my home near Palo Alto, California. The atmosphere that night and a heavy meal is responsible for the following nightmare consisting of a series of dreams.

For the entire sequence of dreams to make sense, it is necessary to explain that although the circumstance of each vision was the same, by some curious mental process, I had no recollection of the circumstances at all. In each dream, the circumstances I faced were totally new to me, and I had an entirely fresh chance to look them over. Thus, I did not have the advantage of working over a familiar scenario.

One thing, and only one, was carried from dream to dream. That was the vivid recollection of the lessons I previously learned. These finally produced success. The whole series of dreams, however, remained in my memory as a connected whole when I awoke.

The Defense of the Mieza HChip

FIRST DREAM

Priorities, confidentiality and file first

Plans are only good intentions unless they immediately degenerate into hard work.

Peter Drucker

Success is a lousy teacher. It seduces smart people into thinking they can't lose.

Bill Gates

I felt lonely, and a little sad, as I looked out the window of my new office at Mieza Technologies near Stanford University in Palo Alto, California and watched through the haze of the afternoon sun in the direction of the successful technology giant I had chosen to leave. It was 3 o'clock, and there I was sitting in my office, charged with running the IP department in a company with only fifty employees.

The company was built on automating important technological elements of the user experience in automobiles. However, its latest invention, relating to what we called internally 'Protocol X' provided the most promising area for potential growth. It was what we called an automotive horse chip (HChip™), an artificial intelligence device that allows a car to refuse to follow harmful commands, like pulling in front of an oncoming truck, in much the same way that a real horse would refuse to be taken over a cliff by its rider.

This would counteract a pervasive human tendency to make errors in judgment when behind the wheel, and was worth an estimated $5 billion annually. The horse chip, by its nature, is both a software algorithm and a microchip able to receive inputs from various outside sensors and to compute, from those inputs, when the commands given to a car by its driver will harm the car and quite possibly the driver or other people. The device contains unique combinations of previous inventions that are now in the public domain as well as new inventions, the most important of which for us is Protocol X, the software and the circuits that create the cognitive brain behind Mieza device. The horse chip is a desirable step in the evolution of cars to safely move people from point A to point B with no driver at all.

Although I didn't understand what it was at the time, I was hired to protect Protocol X and the HChip in which it was embedded at all costs. The company's future hinged upon its success, and we expected to either make a lot of money in the market outright with the HChip™, or see ourselves acquired by one of the technology giants in a short time. We expected that we might possibly face competition in that time, but this was very unlikely, as no other company was known to be within two years of our work on this problem. The competition had researchers on the case, which seemed plain enough, except that the true inwardness of my last piece of information did not strike me at the time.

In the company of fifty dedicated individuals at Mieza, all great and brilliant people, it certainly made me feel somewhat lonely and marooned to be running a small IP department comparatively alone in a boundless field of hi-technology. Yet here with the chance to compete on the world stage I felt, as I am quite sure my new colleagues did also, a sense of bravado. At least here was the chance I had so often longed for when I was just another IP professional within a large bureaucracy. This was my first "show," my first job as Chief IP Officer, and I was determined to carry out my charge to the bitter end.

I was young and inexperienced as a manager, it is true, but I had passed all my studies with fair success and had done well with my responsibilities in the corporate world thus far. The staff who worked for me directly were a good and willing team, with the success of a great enterprise and their own stock options to uphold, and would, I knew, do all I should require of them. We were also well funded, our mission well supported at the top, and provisioned with all number of tools and services to complete our jobs.

As I turned towards my gallant little team and the small company outside our office doors, visions of legal and commercial challenges within a desperate fight to come out on top crossed my mind, with ultimate victory for our company. But a discreet knock on my door brought me back to reality and alerted me that my team was awaiting our first meeting.

Having read the invention disclosures on my desk, I decided that we had enough there to make our first order of business the filing of a patent application around Protocol X and its applications. I knew that a good patent was central to the defense of any invention. Everyone knows that if you are told to protect any invention of value, then you draft a patent that quite well describes its novelty and usefulness in the area important to you. The patent, as I asked to have it drafted, had all the elements I saw required for enforcement. It had a specific cognitive software algorithm and hardware that could not be confused for any other combination, and it was useful for addressing a specific problem, that of protecting a driver and people around him from accidents caused by common errors of judgment (such as failing to look both ways when crossing an intersection).

Given that it was my first day on the job, that the Invention Disclosure documents had been drafted 2 weeks earlier, and no competitor was within two years of our R&D effort, I decided that we could sit on the patent specification for a few days to mull it over before filing.

I decided to explore the offices of my new company, but was for a moment puzzled as to which direction I should take. After a little thought, it flashed across my mind that obviously I should go to the lab, which was where the heart of our competitive efforts lay. It was through the efforts of the people in R&D that we had anything of value to protect and sell, and it is their efforts that competitors would seek to deny. So off I trudged, tablet in hand, directing my steps toward the elevator that would take me down to the labs a floor below.

It was there on the floor below that I passed by the office of Dr. Arthur Border, recruited as one of the company founders. Dr. Border was a tame and surrendered scientist who was the brains behind Protocol X, and his two interns, Lee and Victor. Such a nice man too, with a pleasant face and short dark beard. He insisted upon calling me by my surname, and as any correction might have disappointed him, I did not think it worthwhile to make any. After all, I wasn't so very far from heading the entire company at my position and had received an ample stake of my own in its success. The three of them positively bristled with company loyalty, and the interns showed off that they had their own business cards printed with the company logo. I had not thought to ask about such things, and was much impressed, as the company must think them promising to have them bear its representation.

They escorted me about a lab which had a creative clutter about it, with notes on whiteboards and papers and notebooks. I assumed that to their eyes the seeming clutter made perfect sense. Dr. Border introduced me to several other programmers and engineers that appeared to be thriving here, whereupon several of us gathered in the coffee room and we made up a solid and strong brew. This was most acceptable to me after a long set of days. The whole R&D team appeared to understand IP law very well, and we had a friendly chat, during the course of which I gathered from them that there were no competitive research teams close to where we were on the HChip™.

Dr. Border and his interns took a great interest in my work and asked about how we planned to protect the HChip™. I explained that we would be finishing up our patent application tomorrow and would file it the following day. I was delighted in their interest in IP since IP is what would protect their ideas and their interests in our company. In my past role, it always concerned me when I felt that researchers did not understand or care enough about matters relating to IP. The team asked, and got permission from me, to visit us on the upper floor, and I congratulated myself on the good turn I was thus able to do myself and my company to foster relationships across professional disciplines.

After further uneventful discussion, I directed my gaze toward my handheld that had been buzzing while we talked and the message lines showed me my team was deep into planning the work they would do on the morrow and wrapping up for the day. I walked the peacefulness of the office floor as it emptied, surveyed a wall of modern art bathed in the warm light of the setting sun through the window, whose parting rays tinged most strongly the various tables and chairs within view. The hush of the approaching evening was only broken by the blare of a car alarm in the parking lot outside, which gradually grew louder until it stopped as I approached my office door.

I strolled into my office in quite a pleasant frame of mind, meditating over the rather curious developments that Dr. Border had shown to me for some of the other ideas they had been working to develop. Protocol K had been developed alongside Protocol X for a horse chip, but it used an early generation cognitive algorithm that made it less effective. Protocol G had been developed before Protocol X, and was dismissed because it required communication with a like device installed on the hazard, such as another car, instead of having complete, self-contained function. Protocol X, with its cognitive algorithm, could work well enough independently and represented our breakthrough. Protocol R was similar to Protocol X and about as effective, but the circuitry it required was too expensive to mass produce.

As I sat down in my chair and began to read my messages, I could see that all was well and that my attorneys had things well in hand with our coming patent application. As a matter of fact, one of the more enthusiastic interns had already taken it upon himself to come up and visit and was making a new friend with one of the IP team.

After writing up some instructions on my tablet for the next day, one of which was to finish the patent application so that we could file it no later than the following day, I grabbed my coat that was hanging on the door, put it on and strolled off. The cleaning folks had arrived, so I kept the door open to make it easy for them to come in. I took one last look at the design of the HChip™ on my whiteboard wall, satisfied at the work the R&D team had been able to accomplish. One of my attorneys continued to work, which pleased me with his dedication, and I wished him a good night. At home, I saw that my attorneys were trading notes still, and I was comforted by their dedication to our effort. I finally fell asleep and dreamt of the value of my stock options when we had our patent application filed and our prototypes proved successful. I could have done well for myself in the job I had left, but with Mieza Technologies, there seemed no limits to what I could achieve.

Two days hence, we completed our patent application and filed it at the USPTO as planned. I went about my business managing our company's intellectual property.

Eighteen Months Later

Eighteen months later, I received a knock on my door. "Who is it?" I asked. It was the attorney who had been working when I left the office that night past. He was visibly upset as he walked in and showed me a document he had found. Another company that was working on the horse chip problem had filed for a patent strikingly similar to Protocol X, and had done so just a day before our own. Our competitor had priority on all key aspects of the invention.

I had barely looked at the first page of that application when my phone rang. The number was the number of the VP of R&D. My handheld rang also with the CEO on the line. These intermingled with a string of emails that also came through and the rest of my team standing at my door asking what they should do. At that moment, I must have tripped over my chair, for I knew no more until I found myself sitting in the CEO's office with the VP of R&D beside me, the two other founders, with me dripping with sweat. In every nation that was first to file, our competitor had invention priority, and even where we might contend that we had been first to invent, our claim to that title in the assemblage of notes from our lab was not clear. We could ill afford the time and cost of a contest in court, and investors could ill afford the uncertainty.

In the end, our loss was complete. There would be no IPO and no acquisition because we had nothing of value on which to continue our business that would keep us funded. Our competitor, not us, owned what we had been calling Mieza's HChip™, and we had protected no other means to take our work forward.

Later on, after Mieza Technologies dissolved and I continued my search for a new job, I learned that Dr. Border and his interns had all found jobs at our competitor given that they had no entity in Mieaza against which there would be a conflict of interest. I ran into Dr. Border in the park, and he good naturedly wished me well on my job search and let me know how sorry he was that things had not worked out at Mieza. He seemed oblivious that he could have had anything to do with its demise, if he even had anything to do with its demise. I did not know.

Trudging online through potential new jobs, turned away by my former technology giant employer in my effort to return there, my personal bank account diminishing, I had much to think about despite my torn ego. The rising stock price of my competitor, which was succeeding with all its prototypes, was a continued reminder of my failure at my role and of my contribution to the dreadful losses that the employees and investors in Mieza suffered as a result of my poor detachment.

I gradually gathered, through the grapevine, that the attorneys at my competitor where aware of our pending plans to file on Protocol X and had been in a race with us that we were not aware, understanding the principle behind how the cognitive algorithm should work, to be first to file. I could only be left to guess if their beating us by one day was a coincidence, or if any one of the many people who knew our plans, by deliberation or accident, tipped them off. It has been a phrase I remembered in my childhood that came to me now that "Loose lips sink ships."

As it became more evident that my career would take a step back even from where it had been, the following lessons became evident, the results of much pondering on my failure:

1.   Do not put off taking measures of IP protection till the morrow, as these are more important to the well being of those who work for you and depend upon your success than the comfort of people working late on some strategically important long nights. Choose the work critical to your IP Strategy and get it done so that you are not exposed.

2.   Demand that any record or document that may be needed to prove a point in court for IP be properly recorded in a laboratory notebook or other admissible document.   Include within that document signatures and date stamps that will ease proving the date and origin of the creations.

3.   Do not in matters of IP tell or show people who do not need to know the sensitive aspects of your operation, be they ever so kind or trustworthy, given that people may not even know how the agents of competitors may extract valuable information from them that they may not even realize they told. If people do not know critical secrets they do not need to know, then they cannot tell about them.

4.   Do not leave computers on and offices open without suitable safeguards on physical and electronic files. Never assume that anyone, no matter how tangential their work even on your behalf, will not have the wherewithal to appreciate and communicate sensitive information that you may have left unprotected. Even cleaning staff will have cameras on their cell phones.

5.   Do not, if avoidable, depend upon the validity of one patent for your success, no matter how well written and how sure you are that it will be granted or upheld in court.

After these lessons had been seared into my brain millions and millions of times so that I could never forget them, a strange thing came to pass – there was a kaleidoscopic change.

I had another dream.

First Dream - Notes

SECOND DREAM

Broad claims, competitive intelligence & motives

My job is not to be easy on people. My job is to make them better.

Steve Jobs

Only the paranoid survive.

Andy Grove

I suddenly found myself back in my office at Mieza Technologies on the same day when I started before, with the same directive as Chief IP Officer, and with the same team. As before, and on every subsequent occasion, I had ample finances and tools to carry out my tasks. My position was precisely the same as my former one with the important exception that running through my brain were five lessons.

As soon as I got about my senses, I began to make out my plans for the HChip™ without wasting any time surveying my new office or reminiscing about the company and job I had left behind. At three o'clock in the afternoon, it was getting late in the day, and I was determined to carry out all the lessons I had learnt as well as I knew how.

To ensure that only people with a company mandated need to know received confidential information, I directed at once that my attorneys make their offices and communications secure. They would use passwords and locks and would not leave important drafts or drawings on display once they had served their immediate purpose. I asked an assistant who's desk overlooked the elevator to sign-in people to see us who had not already been given my permission to visit our offices when they chose. If anyone should arrive unannounced, we would welcome their visit, but ask them to request an appointment. I also had assistants scouring publications and interviews that could give me any sign that our competitors were close on our heels.

Having thus arranged to safeguard our IP and filing plans from people who, by design or foolishness, may reveal our important secrets, I proceeded to choose how we would patent the Mieza HChip. I chose to apply for a patent on Protocol X as I had before, which still appealed to me. So long as we drafted it well with supporting data and dates of origin, and filed it first, it appeared the best way to secure the invention. Although it was late in the day and we were tired, I compelled my attorneys, with my help and an order of pizza, to work late into the night to get the job done and draft claims that showed how the HChip could protect drivers and the people around them from human error at the wheel. We had to file our patent application by that next day, no matter how unlikely it was that our competitors had a comparable solution. Too much depended upon this patent for us to take that chance.

During this time, a Dr. Border and his two interns came up to visit to welcome me to my new job, and when I asked my assistant about Dr. Border, I learned he was one of the lead scientists I would be working with and that he had been recruited by the CEO and VP of R&D as the third of the three founding members. Since I had not had a chance to meet Dr. Border, and certainly knew nothing about his interns, I decided it was better not to invite them in just yet while so much confidential information was visible while the attorneys worked. So I left my office, politely met with Dr. Border, and invited him to join me for coffee down the hall where I could get to know him. Maybe he might know what our competitors were up to.

Dr. Border agreed that there were no competitors close to the horse chip solution that we had developed with Mieza HChip™. He was a kind and clearly bright scientist. He seemed friendly and loyal to his company, as I would expect him to be given his founding membership and the stock options I was sure he owned. I wanted his help and his involvement in developing and protecting our IP, much of which he created, so I certainly was not about to treat his charges, let alone him, as spies. As he seemed friendly and interested in my work, I walked partly back with him to his lab in order to look around at that facility myself. There I could see scientists, programmers, and engineers working on all manner of experiments, code, and designs, and could see on their whiteboard walls plans and descriptions of the HChip.

As if anticipating my arrival some years before, within the creative clutter I saw, I examined several of the laboratory notebooks on the horse chips, and all looked in order. I talked to Dr. Border to reinforce how important this was. Locked doors and a sign that said "No Cameras" made me confident that all their activity was secure, which I would expect it to be since what innovator of any sort would want ideas scooped by others?

After visiting with Dr. Border, I returned to my office, paying little attention to the late sun as it shined against artwork on the wall. A car alarm went off in the parking lot, and grew louder in sound as I approached my office until it stopped. I checked my handheld and could see from the flurry of messages that all were working hard and understood the importance of filing this patent application by the morrow.

That night, seeing that all was done, I arrived home late. An absent moon started to rise over the horizon. I lay down for a rest with a sense of having done my job, and neglected no precaution for the protection of our invention and company.

Eighteen Months Later

Eighteen months later, much the same thing happened. I received a worried knock on my door from one of my patent attorneys holding a competitive patent application that had published. My telephone rang with the VP of R&D and the CEO called on my handheld. It caused no small amount of concern for me, but I assured my attorney upon looking at the date of that competitive patent application that we had indeed filed first and would hold the priority on the invention. On any challenge to our being the first to invent, we also stood on solid ground. We owned Mieza HChip™ with Protocol X as a solution for the problem of driver error.

We did not, however, own the HChip for any other potential use outside automotive safety, for in that description our claims had been too narrow and we had not explored protecting what else Protocol X could do.

We also found ourselves open to a host of legal challenges about how specifically we used the combination of Protocol X to eliminate driver error, from sensor communication to the actual mechanisms for overriding driver error, such as acceleration disengagement and brake application, and for that we may have treated the invention too broadly.

Worse than that, competitors had filed patents for other Protocols inclusive of K, G, R, and W and found ways to address their disagreeable properties. So while we did successfully defend our ownership of Mieza HChip™ in the end, we owned too little IP around all the protocols to control the market for preventing accidents caused by driver error, and spent too much time and money to defend even what IP we had.

Our fortunes soured, and I soon had the outmost displeasure to read about our acquisition by a competitor for less per share than I could possibly have exercised my options. Mieza's HChip had been the best solution for a horse chip, but several other solutions were good enough, and our fifty person company did not have the resources to push the HChip through all its tests and then to market, especially while so much uncertainty about its ownership still loomed.

As I put my personal belongings into a box with the head of HR ready to march me out the door, something struck me. Dr. Border had quickly warmed to the new owners where I was to learn he had received a great offer to join. He stopped by my office and wished me well, said it was unfortunate the way things turned out, but he was glad to have made the best horse chip protocol and was sure the new owners would get it out to the people who needed it. "That's what really matters," he said. "Saving all those lives."

Again, as I trudged through Internet job postings with bleary eyes those livelong weeks, I did think over my failure. It seemed so strange. I had done all I knew within my role, and yet, here I was, ignominiously unemployed along with my staff. Our competitor now owned even that IP we had owned when we were a promising startup company. Dr. Border and his staff all seemed to be doing well enough, and seemed to continue about their work with little notice that anything had changed at all. There must be a few more lessons to be learnt besides those I already knew. In order to find out what these were, I pondered deeply over the details of the contest.

How had our competitor caught up to us so fast, and how had they seemed to know exactly how to set up their IP around us?

What a tremendous advantage they had gained filing for patents on inventions we already knew about and then laying hold of that which we held, the very best of all of it technologically, for so little outlay on their part.

Eventually the following lessons framed themselves in my head – some of them quite new, some of them supplementing those four I had already learnt:

6.   Within the entire system that is an invention, you cannot actually protect it if you only own that invention and nothing else around it. The original patent will not stop anyone from designing around it or invalidating it in whole or part. Even if an invention is so fundamentally novel and useful as to demand no further question, it is much better to build a defensive IP position inclusive of related solutions and other parts of the invention system that are its source of energy, transmission, or an instrument of control. This makes it more difficult for a competitor to surround your inventions in ways that limit your freedom of use or to write narrow or broad claims that challenge the full scope of the invention you have the right to

enforce. It would be better to claim related inventions in patent applications of your own or at least to describe them in provisional or defensive publications so that other people cannot own them, and then also to prepare your patents with both broad and narrow claims so that you do not lose out on the advantages of either. You do not want a competitor's broad claim to limit your freedom of operation because you did not claim (or disclose) enough nor do you want his narrow claim to do the same because you did not specify enough.

7.   It is not enough to secure your own operation from the intelligence efforts of your competitors. The entire organization needs to be on its guard. People can falsely learn to expect the facility in which they work to be secure and that it is no harm to tell people who may be friends, acquaintances, or simply not someone in their field, more details about their confidential work than they should. The efforts you make to secure your work must be shared by those whom you serve or it is too easy for competitors to learn where you are. Share with researchers and their managers the common techniques that competitive intelligence professionals use to gather information and make that education a part of your role to protect IP. Teach them techniques like "The Colombo" where a "friend" might say, "Oh, So that was two-hundred degrees to operate," and you correct him with a laugh and so "No, just one-hundred," without even realizing the secret you gave away.

8.   Do not assume that others will equally share the personal interests that keep you aligned with the success of the enterprise, such as stock options. You may be loyal to the stock options you

have been given, but a key member of your team may have other motives, like that of contributing to society. While being loyal to stock options and the success of your company can go hand-in-hand with contributing to society, and so make confidentiality in your best interest while you do good things, confidentiality may seem a burden to a well-meaning scientist who wishes to trade ideas and learn from others outside. So you will need to find other ways to secure his confidentiality. If building a great company focuses the labor of most of your team, you must find a way to align the interests of those who are essential for creating your IP who may have personal interests that follow a different path.

By the time the above lessons had been well burnt into my brain, beyond the chance of forgetfulness, a strange thing happened.

I had a fresh dream.

Second Dream - Notes

THIRD DREAM

Not just patents, but markets

I've always wanted to own and control the primary technology in everything we do.

Steve Jobs

Learning is not compulsory... neither is survival.

W. Edwards Deming

I was at Mieza Technologies on a similar sunny afternoon and under precisely the same conditions except that I now had eight lessons running through my mind. I at once directed my patent attorneys to draft the patent on the Mieza HChip™ with both narrow and broad claims inclusive of preventing accidents caused by driver error and for other potential uses such as preventing operator error in construction cranes. I also assigned them to set up an action plan to protect other protocols such as Protocol K, G, R, and W. They were to visit with Dr. Border and his staff to receive a complete review of their progress on those protocols from which to make a coordinated patent strategy. I closed my door to think about the next plan, interrupted briefly by a car alarm from out in the parking lot.

I cursed the blessed alarm until it stopped. Then I prepared an information and data security process and system for our legal office as before, and set about meeting with the VP of R&D to assist him in establishing an adequate data and information security process for the lab. That would help to prevent the deliberate or incidental dissemination of our work to people who may not have our best interests in mind. Most importantly, I wanted to make sure that the success of our company did not hinge upon one patent for the Mieza HChip even while we did plan to secure Mieza HChip with the best patent we could, filed that very next day at the USPTO.

My plan was thus that we should get the best patent possible covering the Mieza HChip and file provisional applications on other potential solutions that competitors might otherwise use as an alternative and maybe a defensive publication to describe the rest.

We would seek the broadest claims possible for preventing automobile accidents due to driver error and other systems that depended upon the judgment of a human operator, and also seek narrow claims in case our broader claims were invalidated. I confirmed that we had documented well the origin of the inventions covered by these claims in laboratory notebooks that would stand up in court. I also sought to make it more difficult for competitive intelligence professionals to learn about our activities by recommending physical security measures and processes for communication, and also acceptable protocols for publications of papers that scientists might wish to write.

This latter, of course, met a fair amount of resistance from our lead researcher, Dr. Border, who was a brilliant scientist for sure, and who felt it was important to network with his colleagues, and trade ideas in order to create the best solutions for preventing accidents caused by human error. That is not to say that Dr. Border was not competitive, for he was, and he was also highly confident that irrespective of the information traded, he could always use the ideas he received to better advantage than others could use his ideas. He considered our security measures stifling, and I had a long discussion with him and his interns until they had the humor to see the force of my argument, and that security was, after all, necessary for their own success as well as the company. We also set up a plan to review their lab notebooks from time to time from an IP legal viewpoint to make sure we captured the IP that we should.

By the next day, we had filed a well-drafted patent application for the Mieza HChip, and by that week, understood where we were in the development of other protocols and how we would protect them also. I went so far as to ask Dr. Border and his team to work out any other potential uses for Protocol X or alternative solutions that we should explore for patenting or defensive publication that we had not considered. Once completed, we would have a challenging IP position for any competitor to break.

I was astonished, however, with the difficulty the VP of R&D had in keeping the IP researchers that had been working with Dr. Borders focused on Protocol X. They brought to our attention a number of other ways to address operator human error that were not Protocol X. I was particularly blunt in explaining that we needed to focus our investigation around Protocol X. That is where our core IP resided, that is what our CEO and the Venture Capital investors cared about, and that was the market we wanted to dominate with the HChip. I did not want reprisals from the senior executive team for not staying focused, since focus is a key tenet of strategy.

As the weeks progressed and my plan came together, I ran over the eight lessons I had learned, and it seemed to me that I had left nothing undone which could possibly help toward our success. We had patent applications filed on all the protocols we had identified as being useful with Protocol X for the prevention of accidents caused by operator error. We had filed provisional applications or published defensively a fair amount of other IP that seemed less promising but that we nonetheless would prefer that our competitors not patent. We had ample resources and support from the business to assert and defend the IP we had which was well placed to stand up in court if need be. My team continued to improve details around our IP position, including registering the trademark for Mieza HChip. Things were going well enough for me to take a well-earned vacation.

Eighteen Months Later

Eighteen months had passed by, and our patent published without any other prior application conflicting. Just as I settled back into my routine, I received a knock on my door from my senior patent attorney.

My senior patent attorney showed me some reports he had received from his patent alerts. They included patent applications that read on Mieza HChip, although of later priority, and some of the other protocols for which we had filed. That company seemed to be proceeding with their work without any knowledge or concern about our priority patent applications. What a scoop, I thought, all the work they had done and they would soon be surprised to learn that we had already beaten them to the invention. Yes, anytime I wanted to now, we could hop on the phone and tell them their efforts were for naught. We had the IP, and we planned to enforce it.

It was not to be. After a short time, our competitor did stop their research, apparently for consideration. Their heads of R&D, I learned from Dr. Border, seemed to be having consultations at their places of business. For several months afterward, we heard little more of significance. We began our trials and prototyping, and these went off as planned. Our CEO was flush with our coming success, and decided that we would build our own small sales force to sell Mieza HChip. It was clear that Mieza Technologies had the best horse chip and every potential customer would see that.

However, our competitor had not banked his success on Protocol X alone, or any of the other horse chip cognitive protocols we covered with our IP. Another solution for preventing accidents caused by operator error was out there, and we knew about it from Dr. Border's researchers. It was not as good as our horse chip because it used a conventional instead of a cognitive algorithm. It was, however, good enough for all but the most egregious operator error.

Evidently, our competitor decided that it was not worth fighting over a cognitive algorithm when they had a perfectly viable alternative also in development that used conventional algorithms. So they took that solution through trials with perfect success. It was not as effective a method for preventing the harmful consequence of operator error, but it was better than the current state-of-the-art at the time. And it was shortly after that that I received a knock on my door.

"Excuse me, sir. I think you want to see this." One of my patent attorneys directed me to a Web site that announced the release of a new horse chip from a well-respected hi-tech giant. While I focused my eyes on the screen, my telephone rang. It was the VP of R&D. Then my handheld rang with the CEO, and he summoned me to his office on the top floor. After I hung up the phone, I read the press release. This hi-tech giant was going all out to capture the market, from our perspective. Their available sales force was a magnitude larger than our entire company, and all of those prospective customers already knew who they were. Many of the customers, mostly automotive and other transportation and equipment manufacturers, already had relationships with the hi-tech giant for other products and services. It had not occurred to me to consider that anything outside of IP could cause my IP position to fail.

My CEO was uneasy, and so was the VP of R&D. The hi-tech giant had a horse chip, and we were set to compete against it. I assured him not to worry. We have the better horse chip. We called in the head of marketing, and the four of us went through the reasons in detail. When prospective customers see that, they will choose us, and our IP around the Mieza HChip is tight. We will be unassailable.

Days later, we launched our own press release filled with the news about our superior solution for preventing accidents caused by driver error. "Won't this surprise the hi-tech giant when they see it?" Almost immediately, the hi-tech giant answered with advertising in trade journals, in print, on the Internet, and even on TV so that consumers would ask about them by name. Horse chips would, after all, become the brains of the car from the perspective of drivers, and that could foster an emotional attachment to vehicles that people often develop. In fact, users could have their driver profiles downloaded from horse chip to horse chip as they changed vehicles, since a horse chip could be programmed to learn driver behavior characteristics, and so take the "soul" of their old cars with them when they traded into new vehicles.

Our competitor's brand of horse chip and the prevention of operator error became as one in the minds of people, and no one had heard of us. Our salespeople frantically began cold calling, introducing our company and our superior horse chip, and they even made some sales. They could not make enough sales, and we had no more resources to put into the contest. No matter the money we spent, the hi-tech giant could spend more, and each of the sales they made cost less than ours. No one cared that our horse chip performed marginally better because our competitor's performed perfectly well enough almost all the time.

By this time, we found ourselves averting our eyes from the business dailies as our stock price headed downward. Although it had seemed quite a short time ago that all our preparations seemed so complete, now our position seemed woefully inadequate. Each competitive ad and sales call for which we had no answer pushed us further toward insolvency.

I was greatly surprised to learn that no one challenged our IP at first. And then it all made sense when our competitor acquired us. I briefed my counterpart at this competitor about the operations and IP they had just acquired for a song. It made no sense for them to challenge our IP if they felt sure they could soon own it for themselves. The price they had offered per share was not worth the cost to execute my stock options. Dr. Border came by my office afterward and wished me well. He now worked for the competitor and its owners compensated him well. I drove home and began my search for a new job. As I reached out to my network and searched on-line for new listing, the following lessons appeared in my memory:

9. When considering with whom you compete, you must consider not only the technology with which you work, but also all other types of solutions by which a customer could fill a need. When considering these other solutions, the most important concern is often not whether your solution or the competitive solution is the better solution or the less expensive solution. Most important is whether either solution is good enough. Once any solution is good enough to fill a need, then realizing the value of your IP will depend upon other aspects of the entire business that would cause customers to choose one solution over another, aspects of the business that likely lie outside your authority and that will require you to work with others. Having the best or the least expensive solution protected by IP may not matter at all, especially if there are also strong emotional factors that can cause consumers to seek one solution over another that can redefine what is best from their perspective.

10. Do not forget that a strong IP position can become worse than useless to you even if you could enforce or defend any challenge to it legally if the value of your IP position will be determined by a sales and marketing contest, not by the right to enforce exclusivity. The IP that defines your corporate position can both lock your company into selling the chosen solution when customers may have alternatives and allow a competitor to understand specifically how they need to position themselves in the market to win. An IP portfolio offers no exclusivity protection if it does not also read on the alternative solutions that competitors can sell. As good as an IP position may be, it must be balanced by, and align with, the means to market and sell solutions of merit to end-users. The right to enforce exclusivity

on a technology does not correlate with the right to enforce exclusivity on filling a need. There are often many ways to fill a need.

I chewed over these lessons learnt from bitter experience, and then...

I had yet another dream.

Third Dream - Notes

FOURTH DREAM

The race to market and information sharing

Leaders have to act more quickly today. The pressure comes much faster.

Andy Grove

You don't hear things that are bad about your company unless you ask. It is easy to hear good tidings, but you have to scratch to get the bad news.

Thomas J. Watson

Again I found myself facing the same problem, this time with ten lessons to guide me. I started out by having my team file a patent application for the Mieza HChip that next day, and then set in place a plan to protect all manner of related protocols along with Protocol X for the prevention of accidents due to driver error. We prepared all of these with both broad and narrow claims, backed up with documentation in our laboratory notebooks. At the same time, I worked with my team, R&D, and the rest of the company to set up physical security measures for our IP and to put processes in place that Dr. Border and his team were happy to follow, despite some initial resistance, in their own self-interest. I appealed to the professional competitiveness of Dr. Border, and did not assume that his primary motivation for us to succeed would be financial.

So from my office, I chose to build an IP position centered on the Mieza HChip™ and those with related protocols exactly as described in my previous dream, which seemed very suitable for the reasons already given. I then set upon myself to reach out to the marketing department to coordinate our activities, pausing only to let a car alarm go through its course before picking up the phone.

We consequently built a solid patent portfolio and took Mieza HChip™ into testing, but as I feared the possibility that Mieza HChip™, even if technically successful, could face stiff competition in the market, it was a very different plan that I effected afterward.

In this plan, I investigated all the other solutions that inventers devised for preventing accidents due to operator error in vehicles and other types of machines and understood how either Mieza HChip™ or competitive solutions could be better, faster, or less expensive for customers. With that information in hand, I strolled down to our marketing department and asked how we would sell Mieza HChip™ in its best light against the possible competition with our advantages in mind. I sought to explore this broadly, to include the logical parts of the technology we needed to secure with patents to be competitive and the psychological aspects that could be the difference of why people sought our horse chip over another.

While I could not tell the head of marketing what to do, with some thoughtful conversation, I could assert ample influence on his decisions. Through his efforts, we could own the horse chip in the mind of people as the "soul" of the car.

Eighteen Months Later

After eighteen months, as the patent application for the Mieza HChip published, we saw nothing of consequence similar to it coming from our competition. As related patent applications published on horse chip algorithms, we in fact saw nothing of consequence regarding the prevention of accidents due to operator error based on a cognitive algorithm, such as Protocol X, from any other competitor.

Even other solutions for preventing accidents caused by operator error had appeared, however, but we knew about these and could account for them. Although we clearly had the superior solution, we acknowledged that our competitors' solutions might be more than good enough to fill the needs of most users. As we expected our key competitor with the conventional algorithm horse chip would seek a marketing relationship with a high-tech giant, we too sought our own relationship as the success of our trials progressed. If our competitor used massive sales and marketing efforts against us, we would answer with a massive sales and marketing effort for the Mieza HChip™. Further, I worked with marketing to make sure we leveraged our cognitive algorithm emotionally as a way to build the "soul" of a car.

I had been away on a long deserved vacation, and was just finalizing the terms of agreement that our hi-tech giant partner had sent while I was away. While I read through the terms, all that seemed most acceptable, I received a knock on my door. My senior attorney asked if I had seen the news. Our competitor had just launched a horse chip for preventing accidents due to operator error much sooner than we had expected. While I looked at the press release on my computer, the phone rang with the head of R&D, and then my handheld rang with the CEO. Soon I was in the CEO's office with the VP of R&D and the head of Marketing. The VP of licensing at our hi-tech giant partner called and asked if we had seen the news, and with some relief on the part of all of us, he at least still wanted to make a deal. Our relief proved fleeting, however, when he next said that we would have to change the terms and cut our royalty in half. With no other suitors in the wings, we had no choice but to accept his changes knowing also that we had lost the first mover advantage to our competitor.

We announced the launch of the Mieza HChip™ with all the optimism we could muster, but the reality of our predicament soon settled in. A dozen or more of our best potential prospects for high volume sales had already committed to our competitor, and it seemed as if the whole lot of their customers were happy enough with the solution they already had from our competitor not to bother with trying something new.

Even as we cut our prices to try to gain a foothold, an unfortunate affect arose that people now perceived the Mieza HChip™ to be inferior to that sold by our competitor even though all the data showed it to be superior. Our competitor reinforced this supposition with advertising campaigns we could no longer afford to match that asked all the people of the world if they would trust any cheaper horse chip for protection against their own potential operator error than the chip they sold. "Can you afford to put anything less than the best brains in your car for the protection of you and your loved ones?" It was a moral argument direct to consumers that allowed emotion to trump any logical argument we could use for manufacturers who wanted their products to be seen in the best light.

The CEO and his colleagues, along with me, were naturally disheartened at the total discomfiture of our situation, when all had started so well. "Something sickening, I call it," the CEO said. "Our competitor is always a step ahead, sales, marketing, and technology. You never know which way he is going to hit you." To which I could only nod. "We should have moved faster," the head of Marketing said. "If we had been just a little faster, there would not have been the opportunity to cut us out."

There were evidently more things to do to succeed with IP than I had hitherto dreamt of in my philosophy! All the sales and marketing power of our hi-tech giant partner could do little to stem the tide now. Our competitor had the initiative. Mieza Technologies failed to see its investment in the horse chip market returned, and arranged, for a song, to sell its rights to Mieza HChip to its hi-tech giant partner during its liquidation.

Dr. Border wished me well on my last day, and I carried my personal belongings out to my car. Dr. Border had been asked to join the new team where he could continue researching what had been the Mieza HChip™, and received a great employment package. From Dr.

Border, I learned that our competitor had reached the market so early because they had put more good people onto creating, testing, and developing their solution. Their relationship with the giant hi-tech had included research and development as well. I asked Dr. Border when he had learned this, and he said he had known for a long time, but he didn't want to alarm us. As a result, our competitor got to market earlier with a good enough solution, and that gave them the initiative in shaping the market before we arrived.

As I turned on my computer to begin searching for a new position, the following lessons came to the fore.

11. All things being otherwise equal, he who gets to the market first with ample resources to succeed is most likely to win, especially when either solution is good enough to fill a market need. This concept as a whole matters in all efforts, large and small. While we had struck a relationship for sales and marketing with one hi-tech giant, our competitor, appreciating the importance of reaching the market first, had struck a relationship with another hi-tech giant for technical expertise as well. Each researcher had eight or more good hours to devote to the work each day, and so our competitor was able to put many more quality man hours into optimizing their horse chip solutions sooner than we could possibly have matched with our small team working alone.

12. If you change your plans to better compete with a competitor, do not assume that your competitors will leave their plans unchanged. They will adjust to your adjustments. While security measures may

delay your competitor's knowledge about your plans with IP, you have to expect that they will learn about them sooner rather than later. Once our competitor understood how well we were progressing with the Mieza HChip™, its management team opted to set up a relationship with a hi-tech giant that included R&D support. They skillfully managed this relationship to complete their development work sooner, shifting the competition from who had the best technology to who could get a good enough technology to market first. Anticipating that we would leverage our superior technology, they created a strong moral barrier allowing a perceived technical superiority of their solution to trump our logical superiority at the point of sale.

13. Anything that is worth doing should best be done now or as soon as possible. When taking a vacation, which was in fact well deserved, I had not arranged to secure an agreement with our hi-tech giant relationship that I could have secured earlier. Once you have agreed on terms with a partner, he will only come back to you, if conditions change, with reasons to make terms worse for you, and will not come back to you and suggest that he should offer more. Once you come to a suitable agreement, formally lock it down right away.

14. Important information for the success of your business may reside in the heads of people in your employ without you knowing about it. The only way you may learn this information is by asking. Never assume that people, as bright as they may be in their own work, will recognize the importance of information they hold. While you take every caution to teach your team how to keep company

secrets secret, ask what they have learned about the activities of competitors that you need to know. It is no major endeavor to just ask, from time to time, what people have heard about competitors, partners, and customers that might affect your plans. You cannot possibly be more alarmed upon hearing that a tiger occupies your living room than to encounter that tiger after you walk in.

I had no sooner returned home to start looking for new work when I had another dream.

Fourth Dream - Notes

Fourth Dream – the race to market and information sharing

The Defense of the Mieza HChip

FIFTH DREAM

Tackle the entire system

The pursuit of perfection means not just enthusiasm for doing a top-notch job in important things, it means attention to detail and an itch to innovate and improve in whatever we have to do. It means to be dissatisfied with the status quo.

Tom Watson Jr.

In this business, by the time you realize you're in trouble, it's too late to save yourself. Unless you're running scared all the time, you're gone.

Bill Gates

Again I faced the same task with a fresh mind and fresh hopes, with all that remained with me of my former attempts being fourteen lessons. Having detailed my attorneys to file the patent for Mieza HChip on the 'morrow with both broad and narrow claims, all well documented in laboratory notebooks, and to work tightly with Dr. Border and the rest of R&D to protect other cognitive algorithm protocols with patents, patent applications, and defensive publications, and after I had established, with support from the CEO, security measures and security education for all departments, I took a walk about the company to consider other measures to put in place with my fourteen lessons.

I came to the conclusion that it was not good enough to secure the success of Mieza HChip with patents alone, and that if we relied too much upon patents to succeed, then they could make us more and not less vulnerable to failure. A false sense of security that patents can give, after all, can be worse than no security at all. I was quite certain that combined market leverage was in order here, which I understood to mean that the power of my patents would multiply if combined with other aspects of company power such as its brand or a strong sales force, and would diminish if left in isolation. I had seen a pattern I could follow to guide my thinking, that my patent could help establish our brand, and that our brand could then carry our patent further, and that all this depended upon how we set to sell our solution to the market and how we related to our customers, partners, and competitors on all aspects of the business.

As I walked about the office, I got an excellent view of all the parts that made Mieza Technologies work, from our receptionist to our CEO, and upon gazing out on the competitive landscape through the screen of my computer, I could see that even some of the work we could do to expand our IP could also allow us to control the perception of even those who do not have our best interests in mind.

A few otherwise innocent looking patents or publications around the R&D focus of our competitor could, in their emotional reaction to the perceived threat, cause them to overlook the progress of our work on Mieza HChip™ in order for them to focus on what we were doing in their line of R&D. I would rather them suppose that we were years away from an effective horse chip using conventional horse chip algorithms than to make it obvious how far along we had moved with a cognitive horse chip algorithm for preventing accidents due to operator error.

I scheduled meetings with the heads of all the departments and sought how we could coordinate our work. I had to initiate these meeting since for many of the people I called, IP was an afterthought that they really did not understand. The head of sales, in particular, thought a meeting pointless until we sat down for coffee and I explained I wanted to make sure we not only protected the core technology that allowed us to be competitive, but also the IP that could make the difference in a sale. I related a story about car sales where all the science and engineering used to make them master the road could be necessary just to be in the game, and that the difference at the point of sale could come down to the design of the cup holders inside. I needed his help to make sure I protected all of it.

I set up folders to track my correspondence with the other managers of the company. As I logged off my computer, Dr. Border walked in, unhappy about the security measures I had taken, and I began to explain them to him until a car alarm interrupted me. I paused to wait for the alarm to stop, and then put myself in Dr. Border's shoes to help him understand that it was better he secure his great work and let us jointly decide how to talk about it rather than to let his work escape through walls, real or virtual, where he could have no control over it. Collaboration with experts, open innovation, he said in rebuttal, was the best way to succeed. The cross-pollination of ideas allowed him to work better and faster. While I could not argue against his logic from an R&D stance, I could from a commercial stance, and while I knew Dr. Border's primary motivation was to help save the lives of people who would use his horse chip, I could leverage a loyalty to the CEO and VP of R&D who had secured the investment that allowed him to complete his work. I asked him to keep attune to developments from his colleagues at other organizations so that we would have no surprises and asked him to work with me to learn about competitors and their progress without teaching them about us.

Eighteen Months Later

Eighteen Months later, the patent for the Mieza HChip published, and soon afterward, so did those of the other protocols for preventing accidents due to operator error. No other patents of concern appeared from competitors apart from one that we challenged with ease since it neither covered more broadly or narrowly an invention than we had already described. We entered trials and solved all manner of unforeseen technical challenges with the Mieza HChip™ with tremendous speed given the technical assistance and manpower afforded by a hi-tech giant partner that I had signed while our new work looked most promising.

I had toasted the CEO with the finest champagne I could buy at a restaurant that night because our agreement with a hi-tech giant had all but secured the success of our company and our personal success, given the terms we had struck. We had also added brilliant minds to our effort and a first-rate sales and marketing team that would take the Mieza HChip to the market. Each successful trial confirmed our supposition of a successful new way to prevent accidents due to operator error, and Dr. Border had the chance to talk about his work along the way. Dr. Border was further delighted that a superior solution for preventing accidents due to operator error would be available to the public so soon, for he had that sensibility in his purpose for working.

As the day of our launch approached, however, we came to appreciate that our competitor was close on our heels at releasing its horse chip for preventing accidents caused by operator error. In fact, they would launch within days of us. I had learned about this from Dr. Border when I invited him to lunch for a chat. He hadn't wanted to alarm me, and I thanked him for letting me know.

I convened with the CEO, the VP of R&D and the head of Marketing to see if we could move our product launch date forward. I assured them also that our own research around the solution of our competitors gave us hard data to show the world that we had a superior solution for preventing accidents caused by operator error for vehicles and other tools like cranes. Who, after all, would want an inferior horse chip from our competitor when they could just as easily have a better one from us? The head of Marketing set about to build a campaign that would let the market understand the importance of buying the best solution for preventing accidents caused by operator error, which would be the horse chip called the Mieza HChip. He approached this both logically, that we had the superior horse chip, and emotionally, as the place where the "soul" of the car would reside.

A week after we launched the Mieza HChip, with no small amount of fanfare, having beaten our competitor to the market, I received a knock on my office door. I turned away from the window where I had been contemplating just how smart I had been to accept this opportunity at Mieza Technologies a few years before. "Come in," I said, and my attorney opened the door. "Have you seen the press release?" I had not, but an email about it sat waiting for me to open, which I did.

"How can they claim this?" I asked with no small measure of disbelief. Our competitor claimed to have the best solution for preventing accidents due to operator error on the market, which all of our data showed was not true. This made no sense. We could not both be the best on the market. My telephone rang with the VP of R&D, and then my handheld rang and the number of the CEO flashed onto the screen. We gathered in the office of the CEO along with the head of Marketing, and soon had the CEO of our hi-tech giant partner on the line who only wished he could cut our share of the deal in half. For now we faced a marketing fight where our competitor had turned our own words against us. Our competitor totally agreed with us that you should not accept anything but the best for the protecting yourself and those around you when from common human error, and then showed irrefutable evidence why they offered the best solution. Even we could not deny their logic.

I learned that our competitor had taken the idea of preventing accidents due to operator error from a single product solution in a horse chip to an entire system solution incorporating their horse chip. For cars, the predicted largest market, it had licensed a superior heads up display for windshields that could help buyers see dangers better by making the dangers their horse chip detected optically visible to drivers, and filed new patent applications around it. They also incorporated improved conventional audio alerting systems, horse chip-like devices that could read counterpart devices installed on other vehicles for better long range and blind spot warnings, and existing systems that call for emergency assistance if an accident occurs in spite of it all. In short, they gave the car many more ways to communicate with the driver that truly made it feel like the car was consciously out to keep them safe...even going so far as to cross-license an algorithm with GPS providers to tell drivers the statistically safest routes to travel between two points as well as the fastest and shortest routes.

For other markets, they took similar steps. Our competitor worked with safety regulators to show why their complete solution should become standard in all new vehicles and operator tools sold on the marked. They further researched and developed training programs around the specific types of vehicles and machines that would use their horse chip so that customer engineers could help the horse chips make the best accident avoidance decisions for their respective vehicles and machines, be it to attempt to stop or perhaps, for higher performing vehicles, to evade instead. Engineers could know how best to use their horse ships in their own products and could easily model profiles for new vehicles and machines or those with unique configurations. The packaging that contained their horse chip also looked distinct from any other. Our competitor even profited from a copyrighted book and DVD for consumers on how to drive or operate a tool with a horse chip installed, and from an education Web site about how human error can otherwise cause accidents even among people with spotless operator records. Anyone who searched horse chips online would likely see our competitor's Web site at the top of the first page.

While the Mieza HChip™ was the better solution for preventing accidents caused by operator error, its delivery to manufacturers and their customer end users was not so refined, and we left engineers at our manufacturer customers to provide the analyses for best installation that they could receive as a part of the solution from our competitor. It was much easier to use our competitor's horse chip well because our competitor had refined all the stages of its use by its customers, from installation to use by operators, and they had protected all the steps along the way with patents, trademarks and so on.

Customers also felt comfortable with our competitor's solution since so many of them read about it online, and also because it had visual and audio cues that made its artificial intelligence action appear more personal and less mysterious. So while our IP protected a comprehensive product solution, our competitor's IP protected an entire system solution that our competitor communicated to end users as well as to manufacturer customers who would actually buy and install the product.

While true, Mieza Technologies continued as an enterprise, and salespeople ferreted out a place for us in the market where the best horse chip really did matter, we found the full potential of our position severely mauled by our competitor. Despite our earlier launch, our competitor leapt over us with ease. I had protected our inventions, true, but I had failed in my part to make them valuable, or at least as valuable as they could be. Now our own horse chip solution proved burdened by our ownership of it given that we had orphaned our invention out of a total solution for the prevention of accidents caused by operator error. Any enterprise or end user not so interested to build Mieza HChip™ into their own system for preventing and protecting people from accidents caused by human error would have to favor our competitor. And, since most people prefer to make their lives and the lives of their customers easier rather than harder, our competitor's salespeople succeeded much more often than our own.

During the next few months, we tallied the results that had come in since we launched in the market. I took some much-needed rest, and as I walked along a beach and contemplated my future, I had ample time to consider my contribution to our failure and the causes. The lessons I derived from this experience were:

15. A product solution protected by IP may not, after all, though it has command of a technical space, be the best way to command a market. Just as a single patent on an invention can find itself isolated in a network of patents around other aspects and variations of a technical solution, a technical solution can find itself isolated within all the elements that can provide a total solution for a customer. It is not enough for one component of a system to be superior when what matters to the customer is the sum total of how a solution system fills a need.

16. While we understood that the best IP in the world will not matter if no one knows about it, we had not considered that there could be different levels of knowing. All vehicle and operator tool manufacturers knew that they had two choices for a horse chip, the Mieza HChip and the horse chip offered by our competitor. All their

customers, if they knew about a horse chip, knew about our competitor's horse chip and not the Mieza HChip. They started asking for it by name.

We had information about Mieza HChip™ on our corporate Web site. Our competitor had an independent Web site about the prevention of accidents caused by human error that had its own unique feel, plus a special site for vehicle and operator tool manufacturers that customers could go to if they wanted ... and a lot did. It was too much to expect manufacturers and their dealers, even if they preferred Mieza HChip™, to sell Mieza HChip™ to their customers if their customers asked for the horse chip offered by our competitor, especially when the competitor's solution was more than good enough, and as a total solution, perhaps even superior.

In addition to these lessons, another little matter on my mind was what my peers would think about my failure. Lying on my back, looking up at the sky, I tried to take a quick nap on my last day off before I headed back to improve our defenses against expected legal challenges to Mieza HChip™, especially from overseas producers. They would question whether a patent on Protocol X merited the patent protection it received here and abroad, as it was in their business interest to do.

Sleep evaded me. The blue expanse of heaven was suddenly overcast by clouds, which gradually assumed the disapproving faces of my peers. "What? You mean you, had the best horse chip for the prevention of accidents caused by driver error and all the resources you needed to succeed, and you took barely enough of the market to turn a profit for the effort?"

But, luckily for me, before they could say anymore, the faces began to fade away.

I had another dream.

Fifth Dream - Notes

SIXTH DREAM

Getting it right

It is not enough to do your best; you must know what to do, and then do your best.

W. Edwards Deming

I could not understand how it could move under its own power. And when it had driven past me, without even thinking why I found myself chasing it down the road, as hard as I could run.

Soichiro Honda

Once more I was fated to essay the task of defending the Mieza HChip™. This time I had sixteen lessons under my belt to help me out, and in the oblivion of my dream I was spared that sense of monotony, which by now may possibly have overtaken you, the reader. I disconnected my car alarm, which I had found useless to me, so that you would at least not hear that again.

Upon my arrival at Mieza Technologies, I resolved not to contemplate more than the important task I now faced to protect the Mieza HChip knowing its strategic importance to the success of my employer and me. I set about immediately to coordinate our activity with the heads of other departments so that IP and the business would align.

I implored my own staff to work late into the night in order to file our patent application on Protocol X, the cognitive algorithm used in a horse chip for the prevention of accidents caused by human error, on the morrow rather than risk filing our patent application even one day later. We did so with both broad and narrow claims for work that we assured was well documented in laboratory notebooks. We kept all this work confidential so that no one who did not need to know had any inkling of our plans to file that patent application, or knew about our progress at researching and developing the Mieza HChip at all. Although our offices seemed safe and comfortable, we guarded our information. We kept hard copies and electronic files secured when not in use and wiped our whiteboards clean when not in use. We implored that the VP or R&D have his researchers put laboratory notebooks away when not in use and likewise not leave sensitive information on their white boards. No one would be permitted to visit anywhere in the company without permission and an escort, and anyone privy to confidential information would also have signed an agreement not to disclose, teach, or use IP that belonged to Mieza Technologies.

Since we knew that we should not build our company around one patent alone, we developed and applied for patents on related protocols to that used in Mieza HChip™, and in all these patents wrote them with both broad and narrow claims to build their resiliency against legal challenges that could otherwise limit their usefulness. Gathering with my small staff, we created a map around our IP inclusive of Mieza HChip™ and related combinations with Protocol X, such as Protocols K, G, R, and W.

We applied for patents on those we felt had the most promise and filed provisional applications or published defensively those we did not plan to develop but for which we preferred our competitors not have as patents for themselves. We drafted all of these with the urgency and detail that we would if we had to rely upon any one of them to secure our position in the market, given that such a scenario could come to pass.

We also looked exhaustively into other matters of the total product solution, to include how we manufactured and delivered Mieza HChip™, all manner of complementary solutions for preventing and protecting people from accidents caused by driver or operator error, and even the packaging associated with storing and selling the product to manufacturers and distinguishing it from other horse chips. We examined each part of the product solution to document IP as utility and design patents, as well as trademarks, copyrights, and trade secrets. In this matter we took no detail for granted, and it was a welcome sight to me to see each day the correspondences that my attorneys had with people in R&D and other departments, showing me they understood the intent of my directives. They often took it upon themselves to identify and protect good IP that no one else had yet considered protecting.

All of this demanded education where my staff or I lacked in understanding or ability, and so we studied and practiced the fundamentals of our craft, taught members outside our department what they needed to know about IP, and sought our own education about what it took to make the hardware and software come alive as a total solution in the mind of end users. We also talked about IP security and framed our message in the best interest of each other's professional lives to teach how to safeguard ideas and creations beyond the security of filing and data systems to include even the passing of their spoken words to seemingly harmless individuals. Even one piece of information that any individual believed would not give away our secrets could add to all the other pieces that other individuals gave up to adversaries nosing around that could together offer a competitor a complete understanding of our efforts.

I aligned this education with an understanding of the motivations that drove key individuals, be they financial, professional, altruism, or any other personal motivation, so that confidentiality made sense from their point of view and not just mine.

With all this taking place, I considered the knotty problem of what more it might take to protect the Mieza HChip, and realized that building a defense around the central invention that was Mieza HChip™, which is the text book approach to the situation, was not sufficient for our enterprise. The idea that came to me was revolutionary, and against every cannon I had read or heard at law school or in dialog with my colleagues. It was evidently the freak of a sorely tried and worried brain, and I turned away from it until, the more I argued with myself, it all made sense. The more benefits that I considered from it, the less conscientious objections could resist the advantages of the proposition.

The advantages I hoped to deliver with our IP on behalf of Mieza HChip went well beyond the prevention of accidents caused by operator error by methods using Protocol X. They included any method for preventing accidents caused by operator error, by cognitive or conventional algorithms or any other means that could impact whether anyone purchased Mieza HChip™ and allowed our IP to realize its value.

In this market, our success would not depend upon being either the best or least expensive way to prevent accidents caused by operator error unless somehow being best logically or psychologically mattered, two variables that are often independent of each other. We could win if we could offer to the market, and defend with our IP, an optimal solution that was logically good enough and psychologically superior to the other solutions. This psychological perception could depend upon logical evaluations, such as that a passive-to-the-operator horse chip was easier to use and more reliable than a visual or audio alerting system, and other elements that traditionally fell into the realm of marketing around our brand. At its best, it would create a total experience for the end user, the customer of our manufacturing customers, that their vehicle or other operator tool was consciously watching over them to keep them safe, which could build tremendous loyalty to the product...this being a step beyond the original horse chip concept that, like a horse not wanting to be ridden over a cliff to protect itself, was somewhat self centered.

So heretofore, where I saw sales and marketing folks as a strange lot, I now embraced them as pivotal to the success of defending the Mieza HChip, for while I could build the IP position with my staff of attorneys and paralegals, sales and marketing would give that position meaning. I would in turn need to ease their efforts by aligning our IP with the benefits salespeople could sell, here being the cognitive algorithm horse chip for a recognized need, the need to prevent accidents caused by human error, and free them to the extent I could from competitors and the distractions of legal challenges that took money and time away that could otherwise be directed toward selling the Mieza HChip. We could accomplish all of this by expertly executing our craft and leveraging my understanding of theirs.

Now with all of these things in place, the memory of video games from my youth oddly came to me as a reminder of another lesson. When I had mastered the tasks put before me by the game, the computer had a way of offering me those same tasks at a faster pace, and it would continue doing so until my attacks and defenses crumbled. No matter how fast I competed, the computer could compete faster, only now here with Mieza Technologies I competed with men and women who suffered the same advantages and limitations of a thinking brain. The vulnerability to Mieza was clear.

So I and my colleagues needed to look at all we did around Mieza HChip and employ all manner of systems to help me proficiently execute them faster, to include the use of computers when they could speed us up, and the disengagement from computers that slowed us down and appeared to forget who was working for who. We all needed to make our plans around a guiding strategy to proficiently do our work faster for the benefit of the team. All this was to give us the best chance to arrive at the market first with a good enough solution, given the advantage of taking markets while no one is there instead of trying to dislodge competing solutions without the benefit of some enormous superiority in our own solution for end-users that would justify that change.

Speed, of course, was relative to our competitors. Since much of that speed could also depend upon work that only people can do and not computers, more or better staff contributing the quality hours needed to complete our tasks and capture our markets would naturally speed us up. So when our competitor established a viable relationship with a hi-tech giant where we could not match the pace of their effort to research, develop and market a horse chip on our own, we too sought our own relationship with our own hi-tech giant ally that would at least allow us to match. While this is not the only way to gain time, and could in other circumstances even be counterproductive, it was useful for accelerating innovation for our scenario here. I resolved to think from henceforth about not only the material advantages that a relationship could bring, but also advantages in time and any other strategic imperative like geography and the mitigation of risk that might factor into our success, even the possibility that sometimes the advantage is having the capacity to move slower that rivals. While comprehensively managing these things fell to the responsibility of our CEO, my central role with IP put me in a good position to see the whole and influence his decisions.

In all these things that I considered and would consider, I realized we still had an important vulnerability in that our competitor would also think through anything he could learn about us and make adjustments to his plans and actions. I had learnt as a youth about Murphy's Law and that anything that can go wrong, will go wrong. This is especially true in matters of strategy where competitors may look for our mistakes in order to help things go wrong. For this possibility, we tested our plans by taking the role of competitors, and it was through these challenges of our assumptions that we confirmed the importance of seeking a relationship from a hi-tech giant for development of our horse chip and not just for marketing our horse chip. It was an obvious vulnerability once we looked at our position from the perspective of a thoughtful competitor. Upon seeing this or any other vulnerability, it became an imperative to secure at the earliest possible time, given the impossibility of knowing when a threat will test an unguarded position and the likelihood that any change around any vulnerability will worsen and not strengthen that position.

With this also came the realization to me that while competitors could exploit our vulnerabilities, we could do the same to them if that made sense for us to do. To learn about vulnerabilities in either camp, I made it my purpose to talk to a very amiable Dr. Border who seemed, as we coached him how to safeguard our secrets, to know a lot about our competitor's plans and intentions that his colleagues there had freely offered up to him in conversation.

As it appeared from Dr. Border that our competitor had endeavored to develop a horse chip and other tools for the prevention of accidents caused by human error as well, I took a walk about the offices to contemplate the brilliance of our competitor's idea since it could be an important component of a total solution for accidents and their prevention associated with operator error. Our competitor must also recognize the importance that sales and marketing would play in making IP for a horse chip valuable. I saw that there was no reason to limit expanding the scope of what preventing accidents caused by human error meant beyond even installation in specific types of vehicles and other operator tools or the integration of horse chips with more conventional prevention and protection from accidents caused by human error. We could become a central part of the safety experience for the end user, with an emphasis on preventing accidents from happening.

So I met with the CEO and the managers of each department and implored that we take every effort to build and protect with IP all aspects of accident prevention caused by human error from educating people about the causes, to detecting it, to preventing it, and to responding to incidents of potential operator error with the horse chip itself. At the same time, we would secure licenses for the continued development and sale of complementary technologies for horse chips, inclusive of a GPS algorithm by which a driver could chose the safest route to a destination as a priority over the fastest or the shortest route.

All these things could provide for the defense of the Mieza HChip as a way to hold the position and advance it. We would either provide for a better way to prevent accidents caused by operator error than we could with the Mieza HChip alone, such as with a better integration of driver alerting systems, or we could remove a burden, such as by educating the customers of our customers, the general public, on how to drive and operate other tools that have horse chips installed, favoring the horse chip Mieza HChip of course. Our customer manufacturers and their customers would look at us with kind eyes for removing some of that burden from them. We could further work with government regulatory agencies to gain valuable approvals and perhaps make the use of some of our solutions, even the horse chip itself, mandatory.

Eighteen Months Later

When eighteen months had passed from our first filing of a patent application for Mieza HChip™, we had gone far to advance the rest of our effort to create and protect an entire system solution for the prevention of accidents caused by human error that created the impression for end users that their vehicles and other operator tools actually watched over their safety. Our trials of our horse chip proceeded as we would have hoped.

Then I received a knock on my door. An envelope appeared on my desk with a legal challenge to our patent position, one of many I would receive from innovator and manufacturing companies alike. The strength of our position and speed of our implementation attracted a number of lawsuits from people who either had no other way to compete with us or who wanted part of our expected success for themselves. We spent days, hours, and weeks on these lawsuits on behalf of Mieza Technologies, and our IP position held. We later asserted our IP against a venture who infringed our patent claims, causing their company to shut down, although we eventually hired their most brilliant researcher to work with Dr. Border.

Under the cover of a redoubled security program of their own, we still knew that our main competitor would bring its own horse chip to the market, one that we had determined would be technically inferior to Mieza HChip™ since it used a conventional algorithm, but that would still be a good enough solution for most end users if it reached the market first. While certain aspects of trials and regulatory approvals depended upon schedules and efforts outside our own control, we influenced all that we could to move the date of our release to its soonest possible moment, tracking all the while our competitor as it completed its comparable tasks.

On the day of launch, with the full support of our hi-tech giant partner, we had the market for horse chips to ourselves. We offered a comprehensive system solution to manufacturers and their customers for all aspects of driver error prevention, the signature element of which was the horse chip called Mieza HChip™. If a person, manufacturer or end user, knew about a horse chip, then they knew about ours, and while already owning much of the market, our customer manufacturers and their customers continued to choose us more often than they chose our competitor when our competitor finally launched.

It proved all the salespeople of our hi-tech giant partner could do to keep up with the orders for Mieza HChip™ from their manufacturer customers. While our competitor would gain some market share through the sheer effort of its sales team, it would amount to little against the share we held because we had moved first in the market with a total system solution, and the data showed irrefutable proof that the Mieza HChip™ was technically superior in almost every way to prevent accidents caused by operator error than the horse chip offered by our competitor. While logic held that either our solution or our competitor's solution was good enough for preventing accidents caused by the poor judgment of people operators, who would possibly want to trust their life and the lives of their loved ones to anything other than the leading and best horse chip on the market, the Mieza HChip.

I reflected on our success while toasting the CEO and my colleagues. The value of our shares in Mieza Technologies had risen to epic heights, and we had undisputed dominance in the market for horse chips. I resolved that I could still do even better next time. That such a next time would come to pass I had no in doubt, and I would be left to decide on my own how long to continue with Mieza Technologies or where my next adventure would be. My departure would not leave Mieza Technologies in jeopardy for much that I had put in motion needed mostly to be managed going forward. It would be a fine new test for my second in command to try on the role of a Chief IP Counsel himself.

As the smoke from a prime cigar, held by the CEO, eddied in spirals over my head, they changed to clouds of business glory, and I heard over the speakers of the bar a song about conquering heroes.

And then I felt a rap on my shoulder, and heard the gentle voice of my wife say, "Honey, you're going to be late."

In a moment my dream of bliss shattered, and I heard the gentle voice of my significant other. "It's time to get up. I put the coffee on."

I was still at home, waking up to my first day with Mieza Technologies.

Sixth Dream - Notes

Sixth Dream – getting it right

About Robert and Duncan

Robert Cantrell is an IP Strategist at, and Duncan Bucknell is the founder and CEO of the leading global IP Strategy firm – Think IP Strategy.

Robert Cantrell

IP Strategist

MBA

Robert helps clients to develop and optimize their intellectual property strategies, and to integrate intellectual property strategy into business strategy as a whole.

Robert is an IP Strategist, MBA, author on business and military strategy, and a professional shark photographer. He is on the faculty of Patent Resources Group, where he teaches Patent Strategy for Business.

Robert is the founder of Center For Advantage, a provider of tools for strategy, innovation, and sales workshops, training, and problem solving.

Robert has written a number of articles and papers on intellectual property. This includes his recently published book, *Outpacing the Competition: Patent-Based Business Strategy* (Robert Cantrell: Wiley 2009). This book blends patent strategy, business strategy, and classical strategy into a comprehensive whole, with the overall theme that those businesses capable of proficiently assessing their situations, deciding on courses of action, and taking action, win most competitive contests.

Robert is a part of the strategy conversation in the Washington D.C. area, and that has kept him attune to the latest ideas on the topic. Several of his written works are in use at the national and service war colleges as well as in the intellectual property field to include the top selling book *Understanding Sun Tzu on the Art of War*. Robert enjoys the opportunity to cross-pollinate ideas from his and other fields, and then to provide the insight gained as a way for his clients to build competitive advantage.

Duncan Bucknell

CEO, IP Strategist, Lawyer &
Patent Attorney

L.L.B. (Hons), B.V.Sc. (Hons), B.Anim. Sc. (Hons), FIPTA,

Duncan is the founder and CEO of Think IP Strategy. He spends his time working closely with clients and setting the overall strategy and development for our firm.

Duncan is an IP Strategist, lawyer, patent attorney and a veterinarian. He is a Fellow of the Institute of Patent & Trade Marks Attorneys and a Principal Fellow at the Melbourne Business School where he co-teaches 'Strategic Management of Intellectual Property.'

Duncan is also an Associate of the Australian Institute of Company Directors and an Associate Fellow of the Australian Institute of Management.

Duncan is also one of three co-founders of Remarqueble, a provider of outsourced online trademark registration services, and is the author of several books.

www.ingramcontent.com/pod-product-compliance
Lightning Source LLC
Chambersburg PA
CBHW060628210326
41520CB00010B/1511